Psychology

69 Powerful Ways to Influence and Control People with Communication Tricks, NLP, Hypnosis and More

By

Hans Zimmerman

Table of Contents

Introduction

"Persuasion is more often effective than force," – Aesop

"The secret of my influence has always been that it remained secret," – Salvador Dahli

"Persuasion is a science," – Robert Cialdini

My friend, I am excited for you. For what you about to learn is an accumulation of some of the most powerful and proven ways in the history to influence, control and generally get other people to like you and act in ways that most benefit you. These principles are simplified for you here in this book. Ready to start using literally today, to enhance the quality of your life.

What more valuable skill could you possibly learn? Is there any other skill that could positively impact your life most strongly? I say there isn't.

We are deeply social creatures. In many ways our happiness and our success in any area of life – especially our business lives, our love lives, our family lives and of course our social lives – depend mainly on the quality of the relationships we have with people around us. We depend on others to act in ways that help and support us, that help us reach our goals.

There is no more important skill in life than the skill of dealing with other people. Both in terms of influencing people to agree with you, or make a decision you desire in the short term, and also influencing people to change their behavior in the long term. And yet despite its incredible importance, even today this skill is not taught at school. It's not taught at work. In fact, there are very few courses out there to take on it.

But this is a huge advantage for you, not a disadvantage! Because we also live in an incredible age, where the study of human psychology has researched, worked out, proven and explained many concrete ways in which humans are powerfully influenced. Experienced masters of communication have shared their secrets, professors have spent years and huge budgets studying them and breaking them down, Neuro Linguistic Programming (NLP) has developed to great heights of skill, billionaires like Charlie Munger who have developed skills of influence over decades to build their empires are sharing their secrets.

It's a sad thing that most people still do not understand these principles of human behavior, but it's an opportunity too – for those of us who learn these skills, which are not yet widespread.

The purpose of this book is to spread these ideas far and wide. To help you take these skills and tools and begin using them today to enhance your life and the lives of those around you.

With great power comes responsibility. And I trust that you will use these skills of influence wisely. To spread good in the world, and to reach great business and personal success so that you can inspire others to do so too.

How to use this book

This book brings together skills and techniques from many different psychological fields and also practical areas such as sales & marketing, NLP, and hypnosis. As you read through the chapters you will notice that there is some overlap, and this is intentional. It is designed to drum these principles deep into you so that when you reach the end of the book they are firmly in your mind.

The best possible way to read this book is to firstly skim through it. Try to understand the main ideas of each section. Then think, is there any particular skill or system of influence that I wish to use, and go directly to study that section. Then read the entire book through, page by page.

Most importantly, remember the principles and techniques that stay most easily in your mind and go out in to your daily life and put them to use immediately. There is no better way to cement knowledge into your mind than with practical use and early success. Better yet, make a note in a book or journal of your practical use of the lessons here, and continue doing this as you begin to implement them all. See this book more as a guide book to come back to again and again.

In the first chapter of this book, we will explore and clarify exactly what is to influence or control someone. And some powerful principles to remember that will instantly make it easier for you to relate to other people, forever.

In chapter two, we'll talk about the six overriding principles of human behavior and influence. The ways our brains are hardwired to respond to other people, to make decisions. How marketers use this knowledge to make people buy things, and how you can use them too.

In chapter three, you'll learn the most powerful psychological principles of billionaire Charlie Munger, Warren Buffett's right hand man, and how he creates the 'Lollapalooza Effect', a combination of many influencing factors that is so irresistible even Munger and Buffett are afraid of it (*no joke*).

In chapter four, you'll learn the deep power of absolute conviction. How conviction convinces, and how you can develop deep conviction and confidence, so that the power of every word you speak is many times stronger, and far more controlling, making others simply want to follow it.

In chapter five you'll learn the 29 extraordinary rules of social interaction to move any situation in the direction you desire. These rules were developed in the most extensive study of human nature and influence in history. Laid out simply and clearly here for you to start using right now to influence people.

In chapter six, you'll learn the most powerful techniques developed in NLP to influence other people in a completely irresistible way – beware, these are so powerful they are dangerous!

In chapter seven, you'll learn some simple ways to use hypnosis to influence people and change behaviors. The most powerful methods to make lasting change in people's lives.

Excited? You should be! Let's begin by explaining clearly some of the strongest principles of human behavior, human decision-making, and what makes us do what we do every day.

Chapter 1: Why Does Anyone Make a Decision?

"When dealing with people, remember you are not dealing with creatures of logic, but creatures of emotion," – Dale Carnegie

Influence and control really boils down to making someone else make a decision in the direction you wish them to. So to understand how to do this, we first need to understand why people make decisions.

This chapter will lay down some basic, deep principles which under lie human behavior. When you are clear on these principles, you will find it easier to use the techniques in the rest of the book. Because you will know why they truly do work.

The first principle to understand is that human beings are emotional creatures. Our day to day lives are filled with hundreds of micro-decisions, which we mostly make unconsciously, and these decisions are largely based on our emotional responses to things.

No one likes to admit this, but almost all our lives are determined by gut-level emotional reactions to things. These reactions are the decisions which shape our days, and our entire lives.

Because nobody likes to admit that our decisions are based mainly on how we feel in that moment, we almost always explain out decision to ourselves based on logic. We will always give some logical explanation, either at the time of the decision or later on.

This is why you will learn that it is very effective to influence someone using a strong emotional technique, and then help them along by giving them a logical reason to explain to themselves or others by saying 'because...' and giving any logical reason. This is explored in chapter eight.

It's important to remember that people make decisions emotionally, because then you start to realize that people will follow their emotions. Yet they do not necessarily know where their emotions are coming from. You can lead their emotions, in many man ways.

The next underlying principle of influence, is that people are hardwired by evolution to respond emotionally to certain things. We are deeply social creatures, and have evolved that way for thousands of generations. In the past we had to respond *instantly* to certain cues the people around us gave, or we might have ended up kicked out of the group and dead.

For example, if we did not respond immediately to the authority figure in the group when they told us to do something, we could have been in big trouble. This gut-level response to authority is still with us, as you will see in chapter 2. We can harness the knowledge of these hard-wired responses built into people's brains to get them to act in any way we like, within reason. Skilled salesmen and charismatic leaders do it all the time!

These hardwired triggers that give our emotions a nudge in the right direction, and therefore make us want to decide to go that way too. These triggers are actually very useful to use on a day-to-day basis, and we use them today to make decisions more than ever before. In fact, today people are more susceptible to influence by these triggers than before.

This is because these days we have to make a bewildering number of decisions every single day. Even every single hour. Think how complex your life is in modern society. If we stopped to carefully logically weigh up the pros and cons of every single little decision, we would be frozen – unable to act!

So we listen to the little voice in our minds. We listen to our emotions, and we follow those emotions. We do this constantly. We quickly look around for clues as to the right decision (learn about these clues in the next two chapters), we look at our emotions, how we feel about it (learn all about how to influence these emotions in the later chapters) and bang – we make a decision.

Then we quickly make a very strong logical argument to support that decision so that we feel good about it and in case anyone asks. We never admit that we made this decision based on what other people are doing, or because we felt a strong emotional need to do it, without understanding where that need came from.

By the end of this book you will be an absolute master of these principles!

Who can use powers of influence and control?

Anyone can. And here is why. In Robert Cialdini's excellent book 'Influence' he compares using the skills of influence much like using Aikido – the martial art.

In Aikido, a very small woman can throw a large man across a room. Because she uses his own force against him. The man runs towards her and swings his fist – he is naturally on his own exerting enormous force. So using Aikido, the woman moves her weight, touches his moving arm in just the right way, moves it slightly off course so that now his huge force is making him crash towards the floor. Then she moves it again slightly and suddenly his huge force is making him flip over and fly across the room.

She is not trying to stop hum flat. Then push him the other way using her own force. That would be impossible.

Influencing other people must always be considered this art of Aikido. You are seeking to truly understand them – both their inbuilt human nature, and also their individual nature. Then you are seeing the way they are moving strongly this way or that way, driven by these powerful unconscious emotional forces. You see how they are making these decisions constantly, big and small, by looking around at various signals, then responding to those signals. And also by looking inside at their emotions, and responding to those emotions.

Like an Aikido master you are seeing these huge forces inside them, moving them this way or that way. And then with skill and art, you gently reach out and give them one or two triggers and make them feel just this emotion a little stronger – and suddenly they have changed direction and are flying where you want them to fly.

That is true influence and control. As you read through this book and learn these methods, always hold this image in mind – that you are simply using the enormous forces that are already driving people, and are redirecting them a little. To go where you want them to go.

Never thing influence or control is using brute force to stop someone. And then to make them go somewhere they don't want to go. That is not influence, and it simply doesn't work. You would have to threaten someone to make them act in that way. And this book is certainly not about that.

This is also why anyone can master these principles of influence. You are tapping into forces that already exist. And as you learn these skills you will become better and better and more and more charismatic.

Is it negative or manipulative to influence and control others?

The word 'influence' sometimes has negative connotations. It is seen as similar to manipulation. But in reality, influence only means getting people to do what they should be doing, in your eyes. It means arguing effectively. Taking them down the route you want, which you can decide is a positive on for them.

In fact, it's far more difficult to influence someone towards a negative outcome. Or influencing others into doing something they do not want to. Truly powerful influence is effective communication and leading towards a win-win situation, where everyone benefits. It's making people want to do what you want them to do. And then them being happy about it afterwards.

We need influence in all areas of our lives. Anybody in business needs these skills to influence people who have a problem to come and use their services to solve their problem. That is positive. If they don't, then a competitor who has a worse solution to their problem might influence them instead. A parent needs to influence their child more strongly than the local drug dealer, which is a very positive skill.

It would be a sad thing to not learn these skills. Because in the moment when you should be leading someone, perhaps a friend, down the right path, you don't know how to influence them, and the opportunity is lost. It is lost for both of you.

Of course, these skills can also be used to influence unwary people down a path that does not do them good. Unscrupulous salespeople often use them to do just that. So another reason to learn these methods is so that you can yourself resist them and not become a victim. And as to the question of readers of this book using these skills in a negative way, I trust that you are not such a type of person. With power comes responsibility. So please, use these skills for the greater good of society.

Now, it is time to begin with the meat of the book. Firstly, we cannot talk about influence without looking at the 6 key drivers of human behavior as laid out by Cialdini. In the next chapter you will learn them in detail.

Chapter 2: The 6 Proven Principles of Persuasion & Influence

Influencing people is a science. This is the key lesson of the studies of Dr. Robert Cialdini. In some very extensive research over 30 years, including going to work undercover at many organizations who specialize in influencing people, Cialdini outlines 6 key areas of influence.

These 6 factors underline almost all our decisions. We are hardwired to respond to them emotionally, and yet most people are completely unaware of how strongly these factors drive them to make decisions. This makes knowledge of them exceptionally powerful in the hands of an influencer.

They are; reciprocation, social proof, commitment and consistency, authority, scarcity and liking.

1. Reciprocation

When we feel that someone has done something for us, our hardwiring kicks in and we feel a very strong urge to return the favor. Throughout evolution humans have survived by cleanly and clearly reciprocating favors – it is one of the foundations of a successful society. People who did not feel a natural and strong desire to reciprocate would often have been kicked out of a social group. Which in the past, far back in our evolution, meant certain death. This is why the urge is so strong in us.

To influence someone to act in a way you desire, try to think how you can first give the impression at least of having done them a favor. Of having given them something.

The initial thing could be a gift, and this gift can be in the form of a physical gift, a favor or a piece of advice. Perhaps some free information as marketers often use. The gifts or advice need not be too expensive and can be economical and yet, useful to the end user.

For example: by giving a free gift with a product, marketing companies make people buy something. This gift need not be something expensive but can be something of great use to the user.

At the workplace, if a particular thing is required to be done by a particular person, then attaching something as small as a nice hand written note will probably push your chances by 20%. Similarly, sending in personalized gifts or favors is sure to get you in many people's good books regardless of whether it is for business purposes or personal use.

Here, it is important to understand that you have to have your favor returned and if you don't, then it will be your loss. So what you give in the first place should be carefully thought for and you must make it worthwhile to the extent that the other person will return the favor even if he or she is not in a position to. They should take it upon themselves to give you what you ask for and when you ask for it owing to you having done the same to them.

2. Social Proof

We are extremely responsive to what we perceive others around us to be doing. This unconscious function has helped us make quick and good life-saving decisions throughout history. We quickly look around, see what everyone else is doing, assume that is the wise choice of action, and follow the resulting desire to act.

Study after study after study have shown how powerful this factor is. One practical experiment was an experiment conducted where a hotel wished their guests to reuse the towels in their rooms. They decided to put out a few signs, you have probably seen similar signs in your travels.

The first sign cited environmental reasons to encourage visitors to reuse their towels. The second sign said the hotel would donate a portion of end-of-year laundry savings to an environmental cause – trying to appeal to guests' altruistic motives.

The third sign said the hotel had already given a donation and asked: "Will you please join us?" And the fourth sign said the majority of guests reused their towels at least once during their stay. To their surprise, 48% responded positively to the fourth sign as opposed to 38% for the first, 36% for the second and 46% for the third.

If you want to influence people to act a certain way, there are few more powerful methods than to give the impression that other people – preferably people like them – are doing the action you desire them to do. Try to find examples of this to show them, or simply mention in conversation that others are doing it.

Always try to think of intelligent ways to demonstrate this. In business you can always find examples of how your target market is acting in that way. And of course, testimonials are the best possible marketing tool, because of this principle.

This principle also comes across in the weight we give the advice of other people around us – even people unqualified to give a good opinion. So if an office goer is unsure of what he should wear to a meeting, then he is sure to consult a colleague and wear a similar outfit. If a child is unsure of which ice cream flavor to pick, then she is sure to consult a friend or sibling to choose a flavor.

So, if you position yourself in such a way that you get asked for an advice, and then you can influence them to do what you want them to. That is, you can convince them do as you are and do what you want them to for you.

3. Commitment & Consistency

This is by far one of the most powerful forces in our lives when it comes to making decisions. In the short term and long term too.

Throughout human history, it was always important for individuals to appear consistent in their thoughts and actions and character. People who change from moment to moment can appear 'unreliable' or 'unpredictable' which is why we all sometimes end up continuing to do something when we don't even remember why we started doing it.

We also do not like to change course once we have begun. When we are on a course, we start to logically explain it with all sorts of clever arguments, which we then begin to believe ourselves. This cements us on that given track, and makes it hard to change course.

So our brains are hardwired to hold to commitments, and to remain consistent to our previous actions. This is many times more powerful when we have shown our actions to other people, or somehow publically committed to it. This is because it's evolutionarily most important to use that we are seen to be consistent. And it's almost physically painful to be seen to be inconsistent.

In action, you can influence people to act the way you want them to act by getting them to agree and say 'yes' and take very small actions in the direction you want them to go in. Perhaps a long time before you get to the bigger decision you are actually aiming for. In practice, you can start by simply getting a person to say 'yes' and agree that they have acted that way in the past.

Simply by reminding someone that they have acted a certain way in the past, will start to cement their minds onto that track of thought and action. Also, always get someone to speak out loud about their previous actions in that direction. If they at least speak it to you, and preferably many people, they are in a way cementing in their chosen course. And they will immediately begin in that direction and start justifying it to themselves.

Think of a time when you continued doing something, simply because that was the path you were already on. We place great weight unconsciously of our previous decisions. Then, think of a time when you wanted to change what you were doing, but you found it difficult or awkward, or embarrassing to admit, because you had already started down one path and made some commitment to it.

This way of acting is far stronger and more widely spread than we often care to admit. Sometimes people find it impossible to get out of even lifelong decisions, without really knowing why. Like a career or a relationship. And the only thing holding them to that path is simply that they have made a massive commitment in the past, and it is very hard – even painful – to change path and let other people see you doing it.

You can harness this powerful habit of behavior. Simply try to get people to take one tiny step in the direction you desire. Ask them to just say that they think something which is in the right direction. Then after that an ever so slightly larger step will be easier. And so on.

Start small, and gradually get bigger and bigger.

4. Authority

Any attempt to influence someone in any direction will be instantly more powerful and effective if the person being influenced perceives the person influencing to be of higher authority.

Our responsiveness to authority is so hard-wired that it's deep in every one of us. We have developed in status-based social groups for millions of years. For most of human history, if any individual ignored authority, it would often result in death.

This deep unconscious responsiveness to authority is why you always see so called doctors and celebrity figures used in marketing. We unconsciously see them as being of higher authority and therefore their opinion and decision is a better one for us too.

This principle doesn't necessarily serve us in society today as it once did – it doesn't necessarily keep us alive today to do what authority figures say. But it's still there, niggling away in our brains. And you can use it to your advantage by always thinking about how you can give the impression of having authority. This might be as simple as the way you dress.

In one experiment there was a man standing at a road crossing, dressed normally. Many times he waited until there was a large crowd of people around him, then when the light was still red he suddenly crossed the road (when there were no cars and no danger). A few people followed his example and crossed the road with him.

However, they repeated the experiment many times, but this time the man was dressed in a really nice suit – a symbol of authority in most cultures. When he crossed the road twice as many people followed him on average!

This principle is so powerful that generally speaking if you have a very qualified person lying to you and someone of a lesser stature telling you the truth, then you are more likely to believe the qualified person's lie more than the other person's truth. It's unfortunate but true.

This might not only have to do with qualifications and titles and things like owning a posh car or living in a palatial house are also things that people will take an instant liking to and be influenced easily.

Another 'costume' or way of dressing to symbolize authority is a lab coat or doctors clothing. There was an infamous experiment conducted known as the Miligram experiment where test subjects were wired up to electricity, so that by pressing a button people in the room next door could give them electric shocks of increasing power.

Scientists (really experimenters pretending to be scientists) were dressed in lab coats and they asked the actors wired up to answer a few questions correctly. Next to them were participants who didn't know the whole thing was fake with actors.

The scientists asked the wired up actors in the other room a series of questions. Every time they were wrong they told the participant to give them an electric shock. Each time the shock got stronger, and the actors wired up were showing great amounts of pain. In about 4 times out of 5 the people giving the shock kept on going all the way up to high voltage that would kill anyone. Just because the person in authority was telling them to.

Do not underestimate the power of this principle.

Always think how you can apply it. In marketing, you should get testimonials from people in authority like doctors – this doubles up social proof with authority. Think about the way you dress. Think about your credentials. And think about who the person you are trying to influence sees as authority figures.

5. Scarcity

Similar to social proof is the principle of scarcity. We naturally start to desire something as soon as we sense that it is scarce. That it is somehow limited in time or number.

In the past, things had certain value to us – food or important materials or possessions. We would see a thing and begin to work out how valuable and useful to us it was. However over countless millennia of evolution our brains slowly developed a faster way to determine if something was of value. It also watched how other people responded to it, and how quickly the thing was taken and used by others.

This relationship of things becoming very scarce, and of being of great, often life-saving, value to us, was so strong that our unconscious minds can't help but equate scarcity with value, and a powerful urge to have it. In the past this powerful urge kept us alive – it made us act fast to seize the thing. Today, not all that is scares has life-saving value to us. But marketers still use this principle to trigger this deep urge to act and desire something, by making it appear scarce. You can use this principle too.

We see scarcity used all the time in marketing because it is so very effective. Think of a time when you thought you were about to lose something or someone. It greatly heightens the feeling of desire, doesn't it? Or think of a time when you had an opportunity to have something, and suddenly you realized that thing was disappearing fast and your opportunity was about to go! Hard to stay relaxed and not feel like you should act, isn't it?

When you're trying to influence someone, always say something to create a feeling of scarcity. You can always find a genuine reason, in conversation or any marketing. And it's best to give a true 'because' as well. For example, you might say they do not have much time because you are not sure how much longer this opportunity will be open for.

It is vague, but even this will have an unconscious impact on their decision-making process. When you start using numbers, saying there is only this much tie or this many days, or this many of it left. Then it gets really powerful.

The reason it works so strongly to write the number of spaces open on a course, on the sales page, and then count them down as people sign up. The reason this works so well is because it combines scarcity with social proof. And as soon as you begin combining these factors you get what Charlie Munger calls the 'Lollapalooza' affect. The secret weapon of world-class influencers. More on that in the next chapter.

6. Liking

One of the simplest and most powerful principles of persuasion is liking. We listen to people we like. We do what people we like want us to do. Simple.

The interesting thing here is *how* we decide we like someone or not. Who we honestly like in an unconscious automatic, instant reaction kind of way. Some of this may be suprising.

First and foremost, Cialdini says we like people who are similar to us. This is perfectly understandable. We like people who look, sound, talk like us. Who have similar backgrounds or stories. People who we feel some commonality with us, we simply like and are much more open to their suggestions or directions.

As we will discover in later chapters – with NLP and techniques in chapters 5, 6 and 7 – there are many ways to create this liking and sense of bonding and trust through creating a feeling of great similarity. In fact, you can create this feeling instantly with almost anyone though creating rapport. More on that later on.

To illustrate the power of this similarity factor, there was an experiment conducted where a certain number of people were mailed a survey and asked to return the form after filling it.

Those who received it from someone who had a similar sounding name returned the forms more that those who received it from people whose names were not identical or similar. This experiment proved that most people get influenced easily if they find that there is a similarity between them and their influencer.

Perhaps unfairly, we also like people who we find to be attractive. There is a theory, which states that, people who are attractive are also going to possess other qualities such as being loyal and committed and thus, people are more likely to listen to them and also get influenced by them. This is perhaps the least easy principle of influence for anyone to replicate, but it is worth remembering!

There you have the six most fundamental principles of influence and control. If you can begin to utilize and combine Cialdini's factors of influence, you will see instant results. Remember, it is like Aikido. You are not doing anything new, people are constantly responding to and using these forces all day long. You are simply going to be more intelligent about it from now on.

The next chapter will show you more powerful principles of human behavior which will allow you to influence people with ease. And also the incredible power of combining factors all together, and how you can do this in your life starting today.

Chapter 3: The Irresistible Lollapalooza Effect & 10 More Principles of Influence from a Billionaire

The 6 laws of influence outlined in the previous chapter are an incredible foundation to build upon. In this chapter, you will see just how strongly they can used when combined, to create a force of influence that is almost impossible to resist.

Also, billionaire and master of practical psychology Charlie Munger has himself developed a system of understanding human nature, primarily to understand why people make mistakes.

Here we will take some of his key ideas, explain them and flip them over to show how they are in fact some of your most powerful tools of persuasion and influence. It's worth noting that Munger it the right hand businessman of Warren Buffett – one of the world's richest men, who often says he goes to Munger for advice on decision-making. So he is one smart fellow!

The Lollapalooza Effect

When you consider the 6 principles in the previous chapter, you can probably see how powerful they are individually. But once you begin to stack two or more of these factors on top of each other, all influencing an individual to make a certain decision. At that moment you are creating something truly irresistible.

For example, instead of just showing that many people are making this choice (social proof), you could also show that many very similar people to the individual are taking the choice (social proof *and* liking) and among them are people of authority, and also, because there are so many of them doing it there are not many places left and they are going fast (authority *and* scarcity).

Boom – in a few seconds you have stacked 4 principles on top of each other and you can be sure that the person being influenced will be powerfully swayed in that direction.

Munger calls this the 'Lollapalooza Effect' – a massive combination of psychological factors that cannot be resisted, even if you are aware of them. To illustrate the power of this both Munger and Buffett both say they *never* go to an auction. This is because at an auction there are too many of these factors of influence all stacking up one on top of another and even great thinkers like these two would not be able to make a careful, purely logical and calm decision. They would get swept up in it.

At an auction you have authority (the auctioneer shouting out to buy), you have social proof (many other people like you competing to buy it) and you have huge scarcity (just one thing about to go any second), plus several other factors. It's a true Lollapalooza. It's worth remembering if you are ever trying to *sell* something at auction – suddenly all these forces work to your advantage.

Your unconscious mind cannot help but see the thing on sale as more and more valuable, the feeling will simply grow. There are so many powerful influencing factors. It's too hard for even Warren Buffet to keep a purely rational mind in that situation.

So as you learn and begin to implement these tools and techniques to influence people, begin to combine them, but perhaps start small. When you are planning how to express your sales page or what to say to someone, think how you can stack just two of these factors on top of each other. Even two together is very powerful. Then later on you can add more and more and more, to create your very own irrestible Lollapallooza Effect.

10 More Powerful Factors of Influence

These ideas enhance and stack up on top of the previous 6 core principles. Munger highlights them as critical understandings of human nature, and many studies have illustrated and proven their enormous power. Use them wisely!

1. The Power of 'Because'

"A well-known principle of human behavior says that when we ask someone to do us a favor we will be more successful if we provide a reason. People simply like to have reasons for what they do," Cialdini

One psychologist professor Ellen Langer set out to discover how powerful it is to say 'because' and give some sort of reason behind a request. She had surprising results.

There was a queue for a photocopier in an office. Many times she had someone go and ask politely if they could go before the other people in the queue. They were allowed to go first 60% of the time.

Next, she asked strangers to go and ask, but this time say 'because they were in a rush'. They were allowed to go first 94% of the time! Just be giving a reason.

But that wasn't the most amazing finding of the experiment. She then asked strangers to go and ask to go first, and just say 'because I want to make some copies'. Incredibly still 94% of people let them go first! So just because they use the word... because.

When trying to influence people, always understand that like we said in the first chapter, they are making decisions emotionally, and trying to give sense to it at the same time. Always, say 'because' and give any old reason and you will immediately skyrocket your results.

When you are asking a girl out on a date, why not add 'because'? You could say 'because you seem lovely, you like this, you like that, and I want to talk to you more'. Just add in a 'because' with every request and you will become more influential. When you are enticing a customer to by, why now simply add a 'because' at the end of every sales pitch, 'this is perfect for you because...' it can do no harm to give a because, but it can greatly increase your chances of success.

2. Threat of Loss

This principle is clearly linked to scarcity. And it's worth highlighting on its own. Scarcity is more along the lines of making the person you wish to influence feel that the choice you want them to take is not going to be around for long, or is somehow becoming fast scarce.

But threat of loss is even stronger. We are hardwired to hate losing something we feel we already possess in some way. That is why free months with a product work well. When something enters our lives and we get used to it we begin to feel it belongs there, and our opinions about it as certainly far less objective than before we had the thing at all.

Pet shops and dog homes let new families keep a puppy for one day to see if they like it. After that is almost impossible to give it up! Even though you haven't bought it yet.

When you are influencing someone to take a certain decision, always try to find a way in which they feel they might lose something if they go another route. In business this could be a free trial. Or you could simply play on their fear or loss and highlight a problem they have that will lead to their loss of health, or loss of their home, or loss of job or loved one or something else. Nothing hits home harder than playing on these fears. Please use it responsibly!

And in everyday life you can always find a way to point out some sort of possible loss when you are talking to someone. Even if it is not a very logical link. It might be enough to kick in the threat of loss emotional response and lean them closer to the action you desire.

3. Emotional Arousal

We know all about how decisions are emotional not logical. Well on top of that, when people are emotionally aroused in the moment, they are more likely to respond to all the psychological factors of influence in this book.

If you can arouse someone's emotions, you are far more likely to be able to influence them. Just make sure you arouse their emotions in the right direction.

Probably the two most powerful examples of this are fear and excitement.

Fear

As you will see in the next point, people tend to act to move away from pain and fear of pain more than towards pleasure and anticipation of pleasure and reward. It varies by personality, but generally this is the case.

It's extremely classic marketing, the oldest trick in the book, to make the customer feel fear by reminding them of it. Just before you give them the way out of that fear – with the decision you want them to take. This trick is old and still around because it works.

If you can make someone feel fear, they want to make it go away, then if you offer them the way out, they are likely to take it. Especially if you are stacking up several other factors of influence at the same time to push them in your direction.

Excitement

When people are excited and all worked up they simply want to take action. It's a great idea to get people excited, about possibilities, about what's to come, about life. Get them in an excited state of arousal (not necessarily *that* way) and their emotions are leading even more than normal. You will have an easier time influencing them using all your skills and tools.

4. Rewards and Punishment

Just like Pavlov's dogs, humans respond unconsciously and powerfully to rewards and punishments. This factor is very important when you are aiming to influence repeated habits of behavior over time. And as any parent knows, it's the key to shaping the behavior of children.

With reward and punishment, always remember to very clearly and instantly reward good behavior. And very clearly and instantly punish bad behavior. Where good and bad is of course just the behavior you desire or don't desire.

You must be instant because you are training the individual's unconscious mind, and this needs instant feedback. You aren't explaining logically to their conscious mind what you are rewarding. It's far more effective to be instant.

Also, an interesting fact from dolphin training that carries over to people. When giving dolphins rewards, trainers found that instead of giving a reward every single time they did something good, they randomly gave rewards some of the time when the dolphins did something good.

This is because the brain anticipates the reward, but doesn't know when it's coming and gets even more excited. Gambling machines in casinos use exactly this principle to be so addictive. And today, many 'Freemium' model apps use the same techniques to hook users.

5. Comparison Distortion

This is another powerful technique for influence. We all are susceptible to this and it is used against us all the time. On sales pages marketers give an old price, then a lower price, and then a final discount. This is far more effective than simply giving the actual price first time around.

Estate agents everywhere in the world use the trick of showing you a small, expensive place first. Then they take you to the real place they want to sell to you. It always looks bigger and cheaper in your eyes. Even if you know the trick they are using!

Direct comparison in the moment is a very powerful way to make a certain decision seem more appealing to someone. And you can easily use this in any conversation or sales attempt. Simply bring up a worse alternative, then give them your option.

Instead of offering a person one option – the thing you want them to do – why not first try to get them to do something much bigger for you. Then when they refuse, ask them at least to do that smaller option, and they are twice as likely to agree.

Cialdini described an experience where a cub scout came up to him and asked him to spend a few days volunteering for the cub scouts. Cialdini apologized and refused. Then the cubscout asked him at least to buy some cookies. Cialdini bought two boxes, even though he doesn't like cookies!

Can you think of some examples where comparison has been used to influence you? Harness this power yourself when you seek to influence others.

6. Impatience

Here is a nice simple principle to bear in mind. Most people in today's society are very impatient – they want results now. They want instant gratification. They want pleasure now. They want pain gone now. Now. Now. Now.

This is probably not the best mindset to have to achieve things in life, but it is the way most people are. When you are seeking to influence people, use this in your toolkit.

Highlight the instant rewards they will get. Talk about speed and how this option is faster than the alternative. You can always find a way to do this. Combine it with the comparison factor, and find a slower alternative to at least mention first.

A very strong mindset to have in business is to deliver the medicine wrapped in a piece of chocolate. What this means is that a person with a problem may very well need to set out on a long and quite difficult journey, it may take them several years to get the results they desire, in body or business – because in reality most things in life take a long time.

But sales material that talks about a long and painful journey will not be so effective. It does not appeal to the impatience inherent in people today. So you can wrap the good, true lesson – how to get there in the long run – in a piece of chocolate. Tell them the first step takes just a few weeks to begin. Or 6 simple steps. Create the impression of a short time frame, while also being honest. Then when they are your customer, you can gradually train them into being the kind of person who can take the long road to real and lasting success.

7. Drama and Vivid Information

Linked to emotional arousal, people like drama. They become engaged by drama. And they love vivid information, explained and presented in a very sensually vivid way. Most people are far more likely to choose a worse option displayed in a very exciting and dramatic way than a slightly better option displayed in a boring or dry way.

People will often get their imaginations captured by possibilities of a big dream, no matter how small the chances. It's a hardwired function of our brains that when the potential upside is very dramatic and huge and life-changing, we don't make clear judgements and are drawn towards it. For illustration, just think of how successful lottery tickets and get-rich-quick schemes are in every country in the world.

Remember, decisions are made on emotions! Think how you can add a little drama and big dreams to your presentation, whatever you are trying to persuade someone to do.

8. After Success, Comes Over-Confidence

This is related to consistency and getting people to begin taking small steps in the right direction.

When we have had one success, we tend to become overconfident and judge later decisions in a far different way. We are less likely to listen to our doubts and more likely to take risks. And of course, as we already know, we want to continue in the same direction.

Knowing this, it's powerful to give people a small success in the direction you want them to take, before you get to the real thing you want them to do. At least remind them of a success they have already had in that direction. And you are far more likely to get a second 'yes'.

9. Poor Memory Selection

I've mentioned several times already the power of reminding someone of time when they took a step in the direction you want them to take now. For examples, this can enhance the power of the consistency principle.

It is important to note that people do not have perfect memories, with the correct sequence of events lined up in their minds at any moment. As the influencer, you can affect which memories come into their minds. And whatever memories are most prominent will determine their emotions and their psychological decision-making tendencies in that moment.

For example, if you ask them about a few times when they took a chance and had a great result because of it. Then they will be feeling successful, excited and in a risk-taking mood. If these examples were all when they took a chance on education, then it also triggers a feeling of consistency and commitment for them to invest in education – which might be what you are selling.

When you realize you can influence peoples' memory selection in any moment, you realize you can influence their entire reality for that short period of time. It's a very powerful tool to hold.

10. Mental Confusion

This is a big one for Munger. And it's one most people will find easy to relate to. When you are stressed, tired, experiencing overwhelm, or for any other reason experiencing mental confusion, you are especially easy to influence. Everyone is.

If you have ever been on one of these week-long business-building courses, apart from being able to observe all of these factors of influence masterfully executed, you will notice they make an effort to keep you going long, long hours. So you become tired, a little mentally confused and far more likely to buy their big upsell on the last day.

Understanding mental confusion is a powerful multiplier of all the principles and techniques in this book. If you want to influence someone the very best time to do it is when they are tired, overwhelmed or a little stressed. Like all the methods taught in this book, please use this particular bit of knowledge ethically.

Chapter 4: Why Conviction Convinces & the Power of Win-Win

"Ninety percent of selling is conviction, and ten per cent is persuasion," – Shiv Khera

We are about halfway through our powerful and proven methods of influence and control. It's very important to note at this point a very important factor that great influencers always share. Without it all your attempts to influence people will be less effective. With it you might not even need any special techniques.

That factor is *conviction*. The truth is that conviction convinces.

People are swayed and influenced by the people with the strongest conviction – the strongest belief in what they are saying. What they are proposing. When you look into someone's eyes and see absolute 100% conviction to their core, you are going to be influenced by what they have to say.

As so it is essential that you begin to develop this quality, which enhances the power of everything else in this book.

What creates conviction?

Can you remember a time when you felt absolute conviction? Absolute, complete infallible belief in what you were proposing? Think back to that, and try to see what was behind it, that made you feel so strong and sure. Most likely it was a combination of factors.

Many things contribute towards conviction. These include knowing what you are proposing is truly a great thing for everyone involved, having deep inner confidence in yourself, your body language, and other things. Let's take a look at each of these in turn.

How Thinking Win-Win Creates Conviction

If you are trying to influence someone and you believe in your heart that the decision you are trying to get them to take is not the best thing for them, then you will have trouble. You will not have true conviction, and people will see it in your eyes.

When you know in your heart that what you are trying to get them to do is 100% in their best interests, you will have unlimited access to conviction and inner power. You will be calm and strong, and persistent like a bulldog. To take an obvious example, when a parent is influencing their child to trust in themselves, they have powerful conviction. When a businessman has a truly incredible solution to someone's problem, he feels deep inner conviction.

Think win-win always, and you will power forward as a charismatic, convincing, influencing machine. If you realize that for some reason you are trying to get someone to do something that you don't believe is in their best interest, then perhaps you should reconsider what you are trying to do. Instead, find something better to offer.

Or perhaps it is your beliefs that need changing. For example, an insecure man or woman might not feel conviction when trying to persuade someone to go on a date with them. In this case there is no point giving up, but rather work on changing your beliefs so that you realize going on a date with you is the best thing for them.

Developing Deep Inner Confidence

When you feel confidence flowing through you can feel conviction in what you say and you will be a more powerful influencer. Confidence is simpler to develop than most people think. It's simple, but not necessarily easy. And it doesn't happen overnight.

Confidence is mostly situational competence. What this means is that confidence is simply experience and memories of doing well in specific situations. And as you achieve this and advance across many different areas in your life, the effect spreads to most new things you try too.

The key to developing conviction through confidence is to pick some areas of life that are very important to you. These may be areas you are already accomplished in, or areas you have always felt completely lost in. Then set a long term goal to make small wins in those areas.

Take tiny steps forwards, and notice small victories. Pay attention to when you can do something today that you could not do a month ago. Keep on doing this, enjoy it. Become a little addicted to it.

Ideally, make these things something that you are afraid of. This way you build courage alongside confidence. Very few people go on such a journey of gradual, intentional seeking small victories over the long term. You always know when you meet someone like this – it shines in their eyes. Competence and conviction emanates from them. And that will be you in 6 months' time.

Continuously work to develop yourself in general. It is certainly worth making a lifelong study of confidence and building it in yourself.

Conviction through Body Language

Just as we must remember that we are evolved creatures who still have many hardwired emotional and mental processes from 100,000 years ago. We must also remember that our brains are connected deeply to our bodies. Our body language directly and powerfully both reflects and causes how we feel.

Picture in your mind a person who is absolutely convicted 100% in what they are trying to get you to do. They believe in it so powerfully, and excitement and confidence radiates off them. Picture how they stand, how they breathe, how strong their eye contact is.

Now picture someone trying to convince you to do something but you sense they are not 100% convicted in its value. How are they standing differently? How are they breathing differently? What is their eye contact like?

Put the two people side by side. Which one are you more likely to be influenced by?

Even if the not completely convicted person was using very clever tricks of influence on you, it is likely that you would be more convinced by the other person. Just from their body language.

So make a study of body language. This is another way to build self-confidence and conviction.

Two Body Language Tricks to Convey Conviction

As a general rule, every time you try to influence someone do two things. Firstly, before you talk to them, go somewhere private and spend two minutes standing as an absolute alpha celebrating a moment of power and victory. Stand feet apart and hands on your hips, chin held high, chest out, smile on your face. Better yet hold your fists out above you, in the pose of absolute victory.

Look at yourself in the mirror and breathe deeply, enjoy the moment. Feel how you start to change inside. There are studies that prove standing like this actually changes the chemicals inside us, making us feel stronger and more convicted in ourselves.

Secondly, when you talk to the person imagine you are wearing a cape. Stand or sit with straight back, shoulders back, chest out and look them in the eye and smile.

Just these two exercises will greatly increase how convicted you feel and come across. And it will increase your ability to influence them.

Now that we look and feel the part, ready for the task, it's time to study some of the most certain and time-proven principles for skills with people. These next 30 bites of wisdom were collected by Dale Carnegie during his decade-long study of human communications and the secret techniques of famous millionaires, politicians and people of incredible accomplishment.

Some of them will sound simple, but bear repeating as the foundations of a charismatic person. As you read through them, notice how many of them overlap and reinforce the principles of Cialdini and Munger. When you are starting to see patterns emerging, you know you're on the right track to becoming a deadly effective influencer.

Chapter 5: The 29 Foundations of Influence & People Skills

One of the greatest skills in history is simply the skill of dealing with other people. If you want to influence others, you have to possess and develop the crucial skills of human interaction.

The lessons in this chapter are developed from Dale Carnegie's masterpiece of human psychology, 'How to Win Friends and Influence People" a timeless classic crammed full of invaluable lessons on influencing effectively. We will study each one, and specifically identify how it will help you to become more influential in the modern world.

These are foundational skills that everyone should know. A lot of them a grounded in basic understanding of human psychology. Don't make the mistake of thinking you can go through life not taking the effort to learn these fundamental skills of interacting effectively with other people, and then learn a few simple NLP and influence tricks and get others to do what you will.

When you begin to live by following these rules of communication you will find that things naturally begin to go your way. You will become one of those naturally charismatic people whom others want to be around and want to please. A leader if you choose. And certainly, a powerful influencer.

We all know that one of the most important aspects of becoming a person like this is one of the simplest of Cialdini's principles of persuasion – being likable. When you use these foundational skills, and start to study it like an art form, people will notice and they will simply begin liking you more.

Once in this position you will also find being truly convicted easier. All the words you will be more persuasive, and when you intentionally use the strategies of influence outlined in the other chapters in this book they will be the icing on the cake. The extra kick that guarantees results. So study these rules and use them well.

1. Don't criticise or complain about people

"I speak ill of no man... and I speak all the good I know of everybody," – Benjamin Franklin.

In general when we criticize other people, we only spread resentment. You will only undermine any attempts to influence someone or change their behavior if you say anything critical or complaining about them. Don't be like most people and resist the temptation. You will spread a demoralizing effect.

Instead, try to understand people and think and speak well of them. Sit back and think constructively about how you might take positive action to get them to begin moving in the direction you desire. This is not only one of the most powerful ways to become a much-loved and influential person, it will also make your life much more enjoyable. People who criticize a lot are generally unhappy people.

2. Show appreciation, honestly and sincerely

Everyone deeply craves appreciation. Honest, sincere appreciation for who they are and what they can do. It's a deep, driving desire in us all. And at any moment you have the power to give anyone this gift.

Think how powerful that is. And just think how useful a tool this is in learning how to influence people. Practice leaving a trail of genuine gratitude and appreciative comments around you. You will start to have many people willing to help you. And when you make someone feel so good they naturally want to make you feel good in return – remember the principle of reciprocity. Then doing the action you want them to will feel like a gift from them to you.

3. Make people eagerly want to do what you want them to do

Don't just talk to people about what you want from them. Everyone is like that. Instead, forget about yourself for a moment. Take some genuine interest in them, in their desires and needs and life.

It is a refreshing way to see things. Try to change your focus onto the person you wish to influence. Imagine what it is like to be them, and then what are they so desperate to achieve and get – everyone wants something. Then work out how to get that eager desire and turn it towards the direction you wish them to take.

When you understand the other person, you will understand what will get them excited and willing to take action. Then you can begin to frame the action you want them to take in terms of their own life and desires. This will spark genuine, deep excitement and willingness to do it.

4. Start being genuinely interested in other people

The easiest way to become a powerful influencer is in fact to become genuinely fascinated by other people. Think about it, you are talking about meddling in the lives of others. So why not become interested in those lives.

Rather than trying to implement many tricks to move other people. The simplest, easiest way to be the kind of person other people want to help and follow is to start taking such interest in their lives and their adventures and stories, that it is no longer an effort.

People are indeed interesting, why not become a kind of detective and try to work out what makes the people you meet tick. They will sense it in you and all the other principles in this book will just fall into place.

5. Always smile

Sometimes we forget the most powerful tool in anyone's belt for influencing others. The simple power of a genuine smile that reaches your eyes.

Show people that you are happy to see them. That they make you happy. The world is full of people who scowl and frown all the time. Be the different one. Deliver all the methods in this book with a big, warm smile.

Think of a time when you were influenced by a smile. Sometimes that is all it takes. We feel great around people who smile a lot. They make us relax and feel good about ourselves. As a nice bonus, smiling a lot will make you feel fantastic as well.

6. Remember people's names

There is no more important word to anyone than the sound of their own name. And simply by easily remembering someone's name you have given them a powerful and effective compliment.

Why not start every conversation where you want to influence someone by smiling and saying their name loud and clear. It makes everything else so much easier.

To start remembering names more effectively, repeat it when you meet someone. Take a moment to write it down. Really make an effort. Think about it after the conversation. And if it helps you, make some mental images that remind you of it next time you see them.

7. Be a good listener

The best way to influence people is from a position of being able to listen very carefully to them. The world's greatest salesmen and seducers are all excellent listeners. This combines with so many other factors in this book. You need to understand what drives other people, what they want, where they are already going. Then use that knowledge to direct them towards the way you wish them to go. That takes a lot of very high quality listening.

Practice being very centered and present. When someone is talking don't think about what you will say next. Just listen, be interested, respond to what they say. Treat a conversation like a fluid dance, focus on making them feel great about themselves. And gently steer the conversation towards the result that you desire. Always listening, always interested in them. It's a very liberating way to be, and also makes social situations 100 times more pleasurable. It's also rare – people notice. And they like you for it.

8. Start with their interests, talk in those terms

Make it your mission to find out what other people treasure the most, what they hold dearest to their heart – things, people and areas of interest. If you can find out this information quickly, you have the key to all their actions.

You now know the key to their enthusiasm, to their passion. From here you can ignite their excitement and steer them wherever you want them to go. And it's not hard to find out, simply ask them, and then get them to talk about it, to tell you about it.

If you can, influence them by making reference to their passions and interests. A mother might show a child that their hero (maybe a pop singer or a movie star) studied very hard when they were young. What could influence them more powerfully than that? If you are selling something to someone (an adult this time) and you find out they are crazy about salsa dancing. Why not make a comment about how your service will help them afford more salsa classes, or make them better at it, or give them more free time to dance more often. If you are creative you can always find a link.

9. Make people feel important

Alongside genuine appreciation, people most want to feel important. And people can only feel important in the eyes of other people – people like you.

Understand that you have this power, you can make anyone you meet feel important. Make them rise in status right in front of your eyes. In that moment they will value you and respect you greatly, and your words will have many times the power and impact. You will be able to influence them far more easily.

Listening intently to them is a powerful way to make them feel important. Showing great appreciation does too. Introducing them and saying good things of them does too. Tell them they are your most valued customer, and show them the respect that proves it.

10.   Never argue, you cannot win

The oldest, bluntest tool of trying to influence someone (without violence or threat of it) is arguing with them. Trying to change their mind with brute argument.

This is like trying to influence someone as a 5-year old does. There is no point to arguing, if you win the argument you have actually lost, because the other person will resent you for it. And also they will 9 times out of 10 just keep the same opinion anyway. The only satisfaction you get from winning an argument is feeling clever and important for a moment, but at the expense of the other person.

With this book we are training to become grandmasters of influence. It is an art form that requires skill and finesse. So always find a way to change the other person's opinion using the Aikido-like skills you are learning here. There is always another, far more effective, way to influence someone than arguing.

11.   Show respect for their opinions

"The only thing I know, is that I know nothing," – Socrates

As one step further than never arguing, also show respect for their opinion. Recognize that opinions develop over time. Think of yourself a few years ago, you probably had different opinions but you believed them utterly.

This attitude and method is very useful because it will allow you to relax and not become annoyed by the other person's viewpoint. You will make them like you by showing respect for what they are saying, and from this position – where you have appreciated the way they see things – you can begin to intelligently influence the way they think to move them towards the action you desire them to take.

Showing no respect for how they view things will just shut them down and then you will get nowhere.

12.   Admit it when you're wrong

The key to relaxing about being right is being very happy to quickly admit when you are wrong. Quickly and emphatically. This shows honesty, vulnerability and great character.

Yet it's often hard to do. We all have this voice of pride in us trying to stop us admitting when we were at fault. Even to ourselves.

Just think about the last time someone did this with you. How much do you like that person for it? Probably a lot. A great deal of charm is admitting when you're wrong, and a great deal of influencing people is charming them.

13.   If you have a dispute with someone, begin with honey

"A drop of honey catches more flies than a gallon of gall," – Abraham Lincoln

Often times, your reasons for influencing someone will be trying to get them to fix their behavior and come around to your way of doing things. This is often the case in business or in family-relations.

When you are going to confront someone, or if you have to bring up something you are not happy about and try to influence them to change it to another direction, then don't begin the conversation with anger or criticism.

In fact avoid these things altogether. And always remember to start things off with some sweetness – why not? You intend to finish the conversation that way if all goes well, why not start it that way too? The world's most masterful influencers always begin in a friendly way, with a drop of honey.

14. Get them to say 'yes, yes' straight away

This is a super-powerful method of beginning conversations where you intend to steer their opinions and decisions. And it was the trick of the great philosopher Socrates.

Socrates would begin a conversation with someone, and immediately talk about things they agreed with. They would begin agreeing, saying 'yes, yes, yes' to everything, and enjoying the conversation immensely because of it. Then by the end of the conversation they would realize they are now saying 'yes, yes' to viewpoints they had previously disagreed with.

From the start, begin emphasizing and continue emphasizing, that you are working towards the same goal. And that you only differ on the method, not the goal. This way you will loosen up their conviction to the 'method' they have previously held to, and you open their minds to the possibility of changing to your 'method' while still remaining consistent to their original goal. It's a very powerful reframe.

If you remember the principles we began with in this book, getting the other person to start off saying 'yes' triggers many things. Mainly consistency and commitment. They are committing to agreeing with you, and are more likely to agree with you later in the conversation. And also, if you are clever about it, they are saying 'yes' to viewpoints, requests and memories that are all on the same track as the actual decision you wish them to take. This strongly gets them on that track and the principle of consistency will do the rest of the work.

15. Let the other person talk, and talk, and talk

Many people think that influence and persuasion requires a great deal of clever words. In fact, that's not the case at all. It's actually better to encourage the other person to talk as much as possible, because as they are talking you are learning.

You're learning what they are interested in, what they are thinking and feeling. Then gently, accurately, you can use the right words and questions, using the methods in this book, to steer their thinking in the right direction. This way is far more powerful and requires far less effort.

Also, when someone is talking they are committing and investing in the conversation with you, which means they are more likely to want to continue a happy relationship with you, going where you want them to go. And also they are committing verbally to things they say and talk about, so if you can get them to talk about certain things you are doing more to put them firmly on the right track than any amount of talking on your behalf.

16. Let them feel the idea is theirs

There is no more powerful way of holding someone to a new action than if the idea was theirs in the first place. Always try to lead their thinking so that they come up with the idea.

This is another reason to get them to do most of the talking, and carefully lead them to it. The best influence in the world is when the person being influenced believes that they are talking *you* into doing the action that you want them to take.

No one likes to feel that they are being coerced or sold something. It is the skills in this book that will get you this amazing result time and time again.

17.   Honestly try to see things from their position

Don't only try to seem like you see their point of view. Always honestly try to see things from their viewpoint. From their position and experience in life.

Doing this will teach you an incredible respect for other people's models of the world. And it will give you a powerful understanding of people and human nature. When you really, sincerely try to understand their point of view, you will get a great insight into their thinking process, how it was formed, and what is truly important to them.

Most often, this simple exercise will give you exactly the understanding you need to influence them to change their point of view and take the action you desire them to take.

18.   Be sympathetic to them and their viewpoint

"I don't blame you one bit for feeling as you do. If I were you I would undoubtedly feel just as you do," – Carnegie

You can always say this above quote by Carnegie, and you can be 100% honest when you say it. Because it's true, if you were them, with their lives and their experiences, you *would* see things exactly as they do.

Alongside being appreciated and being made to feel important, being understood and having someone sympathize with them is one of the greatest human cravings. Give this gift to people and they will love you for it. And they will be a hundred times more susceptible to your influence and guidance.

19.   Help them feel noble in their motivations

We now know that everyone makes decisions based on emotions and needs. Often rather primal and not always the most noble of needs. But at the same time everyone creates a logical, on the face of it, motive. A noble motive to show the world.

Understand that people have two reasons for doing everything – one that sounds good and the real reason. So use your skills to use their deeper, real motivations to influence them. And at the same time appeal to the noble motive. Everyone likes to see a noble view of themselves, so help them with this image by appealing to their noble motive, and let everyone see it.

20.   Dramatize

We've already spoken about the power of using vivid descriptions and evidence. Try to dramatize any option you want them to take, just like Hollywood. And at the same time make the alternative option seem dry and boring.

21.   Give them a challenge

Simple but powerful. Many people respond very strongly to simply being challenged to do something. This stems from pride, importance and feeling strong. Throw down a challenge and watch them jump to take it!

22. Call attention to negative things indirectly

A great deal of influence is getting someone to stop making mistakes. The best way to call attention to a mistake is indirectly. Delicately. Think for a moment, how can you bring it to their attention in a playful, light way while talking about something else?

The more indirect you can be with them, the more they will be grateful for it and make an effort to change their behavior in future.

23. Talk about your own mistakes before mentioning theirs

A wonderful skill most truly charismatic people share is being able to readily and honestly call attention to their own mistakes and misgivings. And the time to do this is just when you need to let someone else know that they are doing something wrong themselves.

This removes the feeling of being talked down to. It makes people smile gratefully that you delivered it in such a tactful way, and it stops people from throwing up a block in front of you. They will be far more willing and ready to follow your suggestions, right then and in the long run too.

24. Use questions instead of orders

Questions are the staple tool of the master influencer. You can guide people so powerfully with questions, in thought and action. And in most circumstances, people don't like receiving orders. Directing them with a question like 'you might consider this' or do you think this will work?' is a very tactful and strong way to get them to follow that course of action.

25.   Help them to save face

We have spoken a lot about consistency and significance and feeling important. We are very strongly social animals, it is deeply ingrained in us. And because of that a lot of how we act and feel about ourselves depends on how we feel we are seen and appreciated by other people.

There are few things more painful to people than losing face in front of other people. And if you are trying to influence someone to change their course of action, always think very carefully if there is any way they could be seen to lose face by doing so. Because if there is then they may well not do it even if they want to and agree with you.

Take any chance of them losing face away and you remove a large possible obstacle to successful influence.

26.   Praise every tiny move in the right direction

People are hyper-responsive to praise. Remember it well! Never criticize, always praise.

We now know how many strong reasons there are to praise. So praise them on every tiny step they take in the right direction – in the direction you want them to take. It creates a powerful reward for them, gives them great pleasure because it makes them feel significant and appreciated, and it sets consistency in motion. Praise, praise, praise. It's a powerful tool of influence.

27. Give a great reputation to live up to

This is a great secret weapon of influence. We know how important a person's reputation is – how they are viewed by their peers. Well consider the action you wish them to take, the way you want them to behave. Then start to create a reputation for them as that kind of person. You can do this in the words you use talking to them, and to other people too.

Sit back and watch how quickly and strongly they move to make that reputation real. Everyone wants to live up a fine reputation.

28. Always encourage and make faults seem easy to change

Often faults and mistakes in behavior may seem too large to overcome. And if you want to influence someone to get past something like this, their own beliefs may stop them.

But the size of a fault is not an objective thing. It only exists in the words used to describe it. So as you use all your skills of influence to move them in one direction, cleverly use strong encouragement and the right words to make the fault seem like a very easy thing to change and get past. Your words shape the way they think, so use them wisely.

29. Make them happy about the things you are suggesting

This last rule is really a reminder and a different way of expressing many of the previous rules. Always focus on making the person you are trying to influence deeply and genuinely happy to do the thing you wish them to do. When you start thinking like this, you will become unstoppable.

Now that you have these powerful and timeless principles of influence under your belt. Including the 6 basic rules of Cialdini and Munger's enhancements on them. You have some of the world's most advanced and effective tools of human communication.

But no comprehensive guide to influence and control would be complete without discussing techniques from two of the most powerful fields of study in changing behaviors and peoples' actions. NLP and hypnosis. The last two chapters will give you some of the most effective and easy to use methods from these fields without you actually studying them yourself. They are contributed by an experienced and qualified master NLP practitioner and hypnotist. And they are some of the most powerful tools every developed for creating instant and lasting change.

Chapter 6: The Number One Influencing Trick of NLP

Neuro Linguistic Programming (NLP) is an extremely developed study of communication. With NLP by communicating in very direct ways with the unconscious mind – either your own or another person's – you can create instant and lasting changes in emotions, beliefs, behaviors, even values. Tony Robbins and Darren Brown has made the awesome power of NLP very well know. But it is still little-understood.

Most NLP techniques take extensive studying to be able to use. In this book we will cover some basic but powerful NLP methods to influence other people, which can be put into practice relatively easily. These are based around building rapport.

What is rapport?

We all understand the everyday usage of rapport, as getting on well with someone. And this is what rapport essentially is, but in NLP it is to a very high degree.

Friends automatically fall into a state of deep rapport. It is impossible to feel liking and trust towards someone without having some degree of rapport with them.

You know that feeling when you just like someone and trust them, but perhaps you can't say why. They just seem to be on the same wavelength as you, to have the same values and get you. That is your unconscious mind responding to rapport.

When you use the following methods to create rapport with someone, you can create this feeling of trust and liking in them, and in yourself for them, very quickly indeed. It can begin in the first few seconds you start talking to them, and develop over the following minutes.

When you are in rapport with someone, they will naturally, unconsciously feel like following your suggestions, they will be open to you. Trusting and liking. To understand the power of rapport you should know that if you are not in rapport with someone there is no way you will be able to influence them or control them.

All the techniques for developing your skills with people in the previous chapter are designed to build rapport with people. If you combine this with even more intentional NLP rapport skills, you will make your attempts to influence ten times more effective.

Basic rapport skills to influence

To begin with think about how you feel when you are with a friend you trust. You might not realize it but when you have sat down to relax with them, you will be doing many things quite similarly to them, automatically. You will be sitting in a similar way to them, your body will be either upright or lounging, as they are. You will be speaking with a similar speed, and most likely using the same sort of language as them. And you might well even be breathing at about the same pace as them. When you get into all these similarities, you will automatically feel very good with them.

Hold this in your mind as you think about rapport. Because rapport is really speeding up this process, and doing it with anyone you are talking to. When you want to influence someone, before you begin, take the time to talk to them and get into a state of rapport, where you are open and trusting together, and their mind is open to your suggestions.

Matching & Mirroring

Watch how they are breathing. Are they breathing rapidly and shallowly, or deeply and slowly. The best way to sense this is by judging the breaks in between their sentences as they talk. Now try to start breathing with about the same rhythm as them. Begin to match their breathing.

Next, notice how they are sitting or standing. Are their arms or legs crossed? If so, cross something of your body too. Are they leaning forwards? If so, lean forwards too.

When they change body position, just gently try to follow them a little bit later on. Maybe 30 seconds or 60 seconds later. Don't worry about seeming strange, this is actually something people do all the time unconsciously (just start watching people more closely and you will see it). Now you are simply speeding up the process and making sure you get into rapport faster.

Match their language

Notice how they are speaking, are they speaking quickly or slowly? Speed up or slow down your own language to match theirs. And listen to the type of expressions they are using. If they are a businessperson using lots of corporate-speak kind of expressions like 'at the end of the day' or 'synergy' or anything else, then start to use the same expressions every now and then.

If they are very academic, make your language a little more academic. If they are very informal and swearing every now and then, start doing the same. Match them, become like them. Even doing this a little bit will help.

What kind of senses do they prefer?

Just the above tips on building rapport will be enough to make people feel very comfortable with you indeed. There is no need to overdo it, even a little of this will make a huge difference. This next step is for you if you want a challenge.

People tend to lean towards one of four different ways of thinking. Auditory, visual, kinetic (feeling) and auditory digital. To keep things simple, let's just focus on auditory, visual and feeling (the three main ones).

People who are more feelings will use expressions like 'it just feels right' or 'I'd like to touch upon this subject'. People who are more visual will always be saying things like 'I see what you mean' or 'it looks good'. People who are more auditory will say things like 'I hear you' or 'sounds tricky to me'.

Try to notice what kind of expressions someone is using with you, and when you notice if they are using feeling, seeing or hearing words, try to use a few of the same type of expression yourself. You will find that you suddenly feel very connected to them. And they will feel the same.

Leading their emotions

When you are in rapport with someone you will know. You will both just feel this great sense of connection. Then is the time to begin to influence them, using all the techniques in this book.

Also, when you are in rapport with someone you naturally follow each other's emotions. If one of you starts to feel excited, the other person will begin to feel excited almost straight away. And it's the same if you start to feel afraid, or happy, or trusting.

Use this to lead their emotions. We spoke in a previous chapter about the power of getting the person you are trying to influence into a heightened emotional state. Well this is one of the most powerful ways to do it.

Don't overthink it

One thing people overdo with rapport in NLP is trying too hard to copy them. Just be present, talk as normal, listen to them, relax. And generally say to yourself, ok I'll try to match them and become similar to them. And you will find you will just start to do this quite efficiently. That is the best way to start. Try it out, you might be pleasantly surprised at the results!

The final chapter will look at the power of hypnosis for creating change and influencing people in the long run.

Chapter 7: An Introduction to Hypnosis for Influencing

Hypnosis is very powerful, but it's not powerful in the way that stage hypnotists try to make it out to be. Hypnosis can only be used on willing participants, and you can never get someone in a trance to do something that goes against their values.

But it is a very pleasant and effective way to help someone change their behaviors and beliefs, to move them in a better direction in life. Here are a few introductory tips to using hypnosis to influence someone. It takes a great deal of training to become an expert hypnotist, but anyone can use some of the basic principles to heighten the effectiveness of their influence in some situations.

Listen carefully

The first thing to do when it comes to establishing hypnosis is to listen carefully to what the other person is saying. So start by listening to everything that the person you are trying to influence has to say. Pay keen attention, as everything that he/ she say can be valuable to you to use and influence him/ her.

And so, do not but in while they speak and if you have any doubts, then ask them then and there and ask the questions one after the other. Even if you feel the urge to interrupt and correct them if they are saying something wrong, you must exercise a control over your thoughts and speech and keep quiet. They will be entitled to their thoughts and opinions and you must not try and change it as you might lose credibility.

Voice tone

The next thing to do is to slowly tell them your opinion and get them to agree with you. When you talk to them, modulate your voice and decided between a low tone and a high one depending on the words and types of sentences. You must ideally stick to just one, as a sentence with both high and low tones might alert the person that you are trying something. You must also understand the difference between a high pitch and a low pitch.

A downward pitch should be used when you are trying to add authority to your speech. This helps the listener agree with you and can garner an acceptance. Here, the important words that you need them to understand should be said in a low pitch.

For example: it will be "great" if you could come in "early" everyday as you can "finish" your work "faster". In this sentence, you must say the four quoted words in a low pitch while the rest of the sentence can be in high pitch. An upward pitch is usually used to encourage a person. It is used to make a topic interesting and get the other person to perform it faster.

For example: do you "want" to come with me "today" to the "market". The quoted words should be said in a high pitch, as it will help add in interest and encourage the person to join you.

Inducing a Trance

It is quite easy to induce a verbal and a non-verbal trance if you do it right. You must understand the difference and then implement it to influence a person. When it comes to a non-verbal trance, you must have a commanding facial expression and expressive eyes. When you are talking to a person and influencing them, you must gaze into their eyes and not blink. You must engage them in your words in such a way that they can see and hear no one but you.

You must also make use of the voice modulation while doing so, to combine the effects of both the verbal and non-verbal forms of inducing a trance. If you think doing something like tapping the pen on the table will help to induce a better powerful trance, then you can by all means do it.

Inserting an idea

The next step is for you to insert your idea into their heads. This should be only done after the person is in a state of trance and is prepared to do whatever you ask of them. You must share the idea with them in a straightforward manner and not expect them to understand it themselves. They will not be in a position to think and it will be important to tell them clearly. It might also be something to do with what you don't want them to do and you can talk them out of it.

Repetition

It is important to repeat what you want them to understand, so that you make it very clear to them and they understand the severity and urgency of it. Repeat all the key points over and over again and don't stop until you are convinced that the person has understood it. After a while, you will know that the person has understood through simple signs such as blinking or nodding of the head.

Snapping fingers

When you are done talking, simply snap your fingers to bring the person out of the trance. You can also clap if you want but snapping works better, especially if it is done close to the person's ears. The sound needs to be something that will pull them out of the state of trance and yet remember everything that they were told to do. If you wish to better you chances of finding success in the field of hypnosis, then you must practice it regularly. You can have a test subject and practice it on him/ her and improve your skills.

You must understand that hypnosis is very misunderstood and people have all sorts of reservations against using it. In reality, hypnosis is not as dangerous as it is meted out to be and when done the right way, it can be used to influence anybody and get him or her under your control.

Conclusion

The science of influence is one that can be learned and used effectively by anyone. And I am sure you can see it is one of the most useful life skills anyone can learn. If you live in a society, you need skills to influence people.

Always remember that people make decisions based not on logic. But on emotion and feelings and unconscious drivers they may not understand. Then later they explain those decisions to themselves and others using logic.

Always create the most fertile garden for influencing someone before you begin. Do this by making them like you and feel trusting and comfortable with you. Build rapport with them. Come across with absolute conviction and have their best interests in heart.

Then when you have created this connection, use the conversational skills and verbal aikido for the early chapters in this book to lead them strongly down your chosen path.

Armed with this knowledge and the skills, principles and techniques in this book you will soon be a master influencer.

Thank you and good luck!

10477042R00042

Printed in Great Britain
by Amazon.co.uk, Ltd.,
Marston Gate.